W9-AUI-808

Moments in History

The ★ American Flag

By Shirley
Jordan

Perfection Learning®

Designer: Emily J. Greazel

About the Author

Shirley Jordan is a retired elementary school teacher and principal. For eight years, she was a lecturer in the teacher-training program at California State University, Fullerton, California.

Shirley loves to travel—with a preference for sites important to U.S. history. She has had more than 60 travel articles published in recent years. It was through her travels that she became interested in "moments in history," those ironic and little-known stories that make one exclaim, "I didn't know that!" Such stories are woven throughout her books.

Image Credits:

© Associated Press: pp. 48, 51, 55, 65; © CORBIS: cover, pp. 18–19, 21 (bottom), 58 (top); Star-Spangled Banner Flag House: pp. 28, 29

ArtToday (some images copyright www.arttoday.com): 4, 5, 6–7 (right), 10–11, 13 (bottom), 14, 15 (bottom), 22–23, 23, 24, 25 (bottom), 26, 27, 30–31, 32, 35, 36, 37, 38, 40, 41, 47, 50, 61, 62, 69, 70, 71; Corel Professional Photos: pp. 8–9, 46, 56–57, 58 (bottom), 63, 64; Emily J. Greazel: pp. 12, 13 (top), 15 (top)(center), 16, 20, 21 (top), 25 (top), 33, 42, 43, 59, 68; Library of Congress: pp. 34, 52, 53; National Archives: pp. 6–7 (left), 39.

Table of Contents

A Timeline of Important Events

1497	English explorer John Cabot comes to North America, bringing the red and white flag of St. George.
1607	English settlers at Jamestown fly the flag of St. George. Some of them fly Britain's newer flag, the Union Jack.
1707	English settlers **adopt** the new Red Ensign flag.
1775	Ships of the Continental Navy fly several kinds of flags. The pine tree and the rattlesnake are popular symbols. On December 3, John Paul Jones raises the Continental Colors over his ship. It is the first flag to fly over an American warship.
1776	On January 1, the Continental Colors fly over George Washington's headquarters at Cambridge, Massachusetts. According to legend, Betsy Ross makes the first American flag. The American flag receives its first foreign salute—at Fort Orange in the Dutch West Indies.

1777	On June 14, the Continental Congress passes America's first flag law.
1778	The French salute the American flag flying over John Paul Jones's ship, *Ranger*.
1779	John Paul Jones, flying a flag with red, white, and blue stripes, takes a fleet of American ships into battle against the British.
1780	Francis Hopkinson claims to have designed the first American flag.
1787–1790	An American merchant ship, *Columbia*, sails around the world flying the Stars and Stripes.
1791	Vermont joins the United States.
1792	Kentucky is admitted to the United States.
1794	On January 13, Congress passes a second flag law. The flag would have 15 stars and 15 stripes as of May 1795.
1804–1805	Lewis and Clark carry the 15-star flag on their expedition to the Pacific Coast.
1814	During the battle of Lake Erie, Commander Oliver H. Perry flies a flag over his vessel that reads "Don't Give Up the Ship." Mary Pickersgill makes a 15-star flag for Fort McHenry in Baltimore's harbor. During a battle the night of September 13–14, Francis Scott Key writes a poem about the flag at Fort McHenry.

Francis Scott Key

1818	On April 4, Congress passes a new flag law setting the number of stars and stripes.
	Stars for Tennessee, Ohio, Louisiana, Indiana, and Mississippi are added to the flag.
1819–1822	Congress orders stars for four new states. Illinois and Maine will be free states. Alabama and Missouri will allow slavery.
1824	William Driver names his flag "Old Glory."
1836–1851	Arkansas, Michigan, Florida, Texas, Iowa, Wisconsin, and California add stars to Old Glory.
1853	Matthew Perry sails into Tokyo Bay to show America's **might**.
1858–1859	Stars for Minnesota and Oregon are added to the flag.
1860	Abraham Lincoln is elected president. In December, South Carolina **secedes**. Six other states soon follow.

1861	Southern forces fire upon Fort Sumter. More southern states secede, making a total of 11.
	In March, the Confederacy adopts its first flag, the Stars and Bars.
	On June 14, the state of Connecticut observes a special day to honor the Stars and Stripes
	In July, the Confederacy flies its battle flag.
1861–1863	Stars for Kansas and West Virginia are added to the Stars and Stripes.
1863	In May, the Confederacy adopts another flag.
1865	In February, the Confederacy adds a red stripe to the edge of its 1863 flag.
	On April 9, the Civil War ends.
	On April 14, President Lincoln is **assassinated**.
	On July 4, the state of Nevada adds its star to Old Glory.
1867	Nebraska becomes a state.
1868	Decoration Day is first observed on May 30.
1876	Colorado becomes the "Centennial State" by adding its star on the one hundredth birthday of the United States.

1877	Flag Day is first observed nationwide in the United States. It marks the 100th anniversary of the original resolution.
1885	Teacher B. J. Cigrand observes Flag Day with his students.
1890	Five stars are added to the Stars and Stripes. They stand for North Dakota, South Dakota, Montana, Washington, and Idaho.
1891	The star for Wyoming is added.
1892	Boston editor Francis Bellamy and patriot James B. Upham write the Pledge of Allegiance.
1896	The star for Utah is added.
1898	The U.S. declares war against Spain. The fighting continues for 114 days.
1905	President Theodore Roosevelt orders that Civil War battle flags be returned to the southern states.
1907–1909	A fleet of U.S. ships sails around the world flying the Stars and Stripes.
1908	Oklahoma, a longtime Indian territory, becomes a state.
1909	On April 6, Robert E. Peary reaches the North Pole and marks it with the American flag.
1912	Stars for New Mexico and Arizona are added to the flag.

1916	President Woodrow Wilson proclaims June 14 as an annual flag day.
1926	Admiral Richard E. Byrd flies over the North Pole and drops an American flag. In 1929, Byrd and his chief pilot fly to the South Pole.
1945	On February 23, U.S. Marines raise the American flag on Iwo Jima.
1959	Alaska becomes a state.
1960	Hawaii becomes a state.
1969	On July 20, astronauts Neil Armstrong and Buzz Aldrin place an American flag on the moon.
2001	On September 11, terrorists attack New York City and Washington, D.C. Americans unite around their flag with new respect.

A History of Flags

Many thousands of years ago, men going to war held up symbols and brightly colored pieces of cloth. Sometimes they tied streamers to the tops of long poles. They did these things to honor the gods they worshiped. And they wanted others to know which state or kingdom they were from.

The first people to do this were the Egyptians. Their flags were streamers on poles. On top of each pole was the fanlike symbol that stood for the **pharaohs**. Later the Assyrians, Greeks, and Romans used flags. Their symbols sometimes stood for gods. Other times, the symbols stood for the countries' leaders.

Cloth flags, such as the ones we know today, were first used in China and India. Often they were made of silk and showed pictures of tigers and dragons.

Early flags were held high in battle. Officers could find their warriors by

Egyptians holding flags that honor the pharaoh

10

looking for the right flag. And soldiers separated from their units could go toward the flags and find their countrymen.

Flags had another use in the days of bows and arrows. Arrows would not travel straight when winds were strong. So archers looked up at the flags to see which way the wind was blowing. This helped them aim.

Long ago, during a period called the Middle Ages, seven colors became common on flags. They were red, white, blue, green, yellow, black, and orange. Even today you will have to look carefully to find other colors on the flag of any nation.

The word *flag* comes from an old English word *fleogan*. The term means "to fly in the wind."

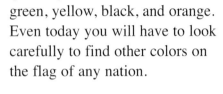

2 Patriots in Search of a Flag

The explorer John Cabot came to North America from England in 1497. He carried his country's flag with him. The background, or **field**, was white. On it was the red cross of St. George, an English hero in a myth about dragons.

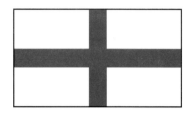

Flag of St. George

English settlers arrived at Jamestown, in what is now the state of Virginia, 110 years later. They, too, flew the red and white flag of St. George.

But it is also likely that these settlers brought the Union Jack. This was the flag that England had adopted just one year before when England and Scotland joined to become one country. The Union Jack showed the cross of St. George and the X-shaped cross of St. Andrew, the hero of Scotland. The flag was red, white, and blue—the colors used later to make the American flag.

Union Jack

England's ships flew another flag. The Red Ensign, also called the Red Meteor, flew from each vessel. Its **canton**, a section in the upper-left corner, showed St. George's cross on a white background. The field for the rest of the flag was red.

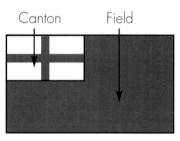

Canton   Field

Red Ensign (Red Meteor)

In 1707, a new Red Ensign was introduced. For this flag, the field remained red. The canton, however, was the Union Jack, with the crosses of St. George and St. Andrew on a blue background.

New Red Ensign

The 13 colonies in the New World belonged to England. So the two flags—the Union Jack and the Red Ensign—flew from ship masts and flagpoles in all of the colonies.

In the early 1700s, the colonists in America began to complain about the English government. They did not like the way England treated her 13 colonies.

King George III of England demanded high taxes. Most settlers did not want to pay such taxes. But many of them did not want to break away from the mother country either.

King George III of England

War Comes Near

Disagreements between England and the colonies continued. From time to time in 1775, fighting broke out. Brave settlers, or **patriots**, were willing to fight for what they believed. And they believed that the colonies should have the right to decide more things for themselves.

An angry battle was fought in the villages of Lexington and Concord in Massachusetts. And in Boston, with only a few minutes to get ready, thousands of young patriots, known as "minutemen," rushed to battle. Bravely, they fought against the English at a place called Bunker Hill. Unfortunately, there are no clear records of which flags, if any, flew over the patriots in those battles.

In the fall of 1775, the members of the Continental Congress met. Men **representing** each of the 13 colonies talked and planned for more than 12 hours a day. There was much to decide and no time in such busy sessions to talk about flags.

The Continental Congress named George Washington, a Virginia **planter**, commander in chief of all the patriot forces. Soon, Washington had formed the Continental Navy. A limited war at sea began.

George Washington

14

But there was no flag for the united colonies. How would the captains of ships know one another? How would ships of other countries recognize the colonial fleet?

Many New England colonies had designed their own flags. One popular symbol on these flags was a pine tree on a field of white. Most of the ships in the new navy were from New England. So it made sense to use the

AN APPEAL TO HEAVEN

Pine tree flag

pine tree on the first flags flown from American warships.

The flags were not all exactly alike, but they were similar. On each, either above or below the green pine tree, were the words "An Appeal to Heaven." These words showed that the colonists believed God would see their cause as a just one. For a few months in 1775, these pine-tree flags were all that identified the Continental Navy and its few ships.

Later that same year, some patriots began using a striped flag with a rattlesnake design. In South Carolina, the words under the snake said, "Don't **Tread** on Me."

In December of 1775, ships of the

DON'T TREAD ON ME

Rattlesnake flag

new Continental fleet sailed out of Philadelphia under the command of Commodore Esek Hopkins. On the **flagship** carrying Hopkins was a 28-year-old officer who would become famous for his bravery in battle. His name was John Paul Jones. Reckless in his earlier days, young Jones was now ready to be a leader.

Esek Hopkins

15

According to the diary of John Paul Jones, on December 3, 1775, he unfurled a new flag in Philadelphia's harbor. It was called the Continental Colors. Its 13 stripes represented not just one colony but all 13 colonies.

Continental Colors

One thing made the Continental Colors different from the Red Ensign. Six white stripes ran across the red field. Now there was a total of 13 stripes, with red ones at the top and bottom. The canton remained the same, still representing England with the Union Jack.

When Jones raised the Continental Colors to the **masthead** of his ship, it became the first flag to fly over the first ship in what would later be known as the United States Navy.

John Paul Jones knew this new flag was more important than the pine tree flag. It was more important than the rattlesnake flag. Because it stood for *all* patriots.

This flag was called by more than one name. Besides the Continental Colors, it was known as the Grand Union Flag and the Great Union Flag.

Four weeks later, on January 1, 1776, the new flag was raised over General George Washington's headquarters at Cambridge, Massachusetts.

For a year and a half, this flag, with its reminders of England, served as the symbol of the united colonies.

The Legend of Betsy Ross 3

On July 4, 1776, the members of the Continental
Congress finished writing the words that united the new
country. The 13 colonies had pledged to become a new
nation. But there was still no national flag—one that did not
bear English symbols.

> The original 13 states were
> Delaware, Connecticut, Georgia,
> Maryland, Massachusetts,
> New Hampshire, New Jersey,
> New York, North Carolina,
> Pennsylvania, Rhode Island,
> South Carolina, and Virginia.

Most Americans know of the
widow Mrs. Elizabeth (Betsy)
Ross of Philadelphia. Throughout
history, she has been known as the
woman who sewed the first United
States flag. As the story goes, she
was asked to do this by General
George Washington.

This story was not made
public for almost 100 years. In
1870, Mrs. Ross's grandson,
William J. Canby, gave a speech
to the Pennsylvania Historical Society. In it, he claimed that
his grandmother had made the first American flag. No one
had heard this claim before.

The original 13 states

17

As Canby's story goes, in June of 1776, a committee of important men visited Mrs. Ross's **upholstery** shop. One of the men was Colonel George Ross, an uncle of Betsy's deceased husband. Another was Robert Morris, a rich politician. The third man, Canby claimed in his speech, was General George Washington.

The men said they knew Betsy Ross was a fine seamstress. They wanted a flag. Could she make one for them?

Betsy Ross, her grandson said, had never made a flag. But she was willing to try. The visitors made a rough drawing of what they wanted.

Mrs. Ross looked at the drawing. She suggested some changes. George Washington was reported to have listened carefully. Then he drew a new design. It was a flag having a field of 13 stripes. That part looked like the Grand Union flag.

The canton, however, did not have the British Union Jack. Instead, it contained 13 six-pointed stars in a circle. Betsy Ross showed General Washington how to cut stars with five points. She told him they would look better.

Betsy Ross and George Washington

The story of Betsy Ross's meeting with General Washington and the other two men is a charming one. However, there is nothing in history that backs it up. Very few historians believe it happened.

There *was* a Betsy Ross. And later in the Revolutionary War, she did make flags. But there is no record that she made the first Stars and Stripes. And there is no record that someone else did it that June either.

In fact, the members of the Continental Congress had not yet voted for independence. Records show that George Washington was in Philadelphia in June 1776. But by the time the 13 colonies voted to unite on July 4, he had left the city.

Today, you can visit the small home of Betsy Ross in Philadelphia. It has been restored to look the way it did in 1776. The story about her flag, true or not, is one Americans will never forget.

Another Claim

A different person who claimed to have designed the flag was Francis Hopkinson. He was a poet, an artist, and a congressman from the state of New Jersey. He had designed the seal that stood for New Jersey and another for the American Board of Admiralty.

In 1780, Hopkinson wrote a letter, claiming to have designed "The Flag of the United States of America." He asked for no pay.

Later, he changed his mind. He sent a bill to Congress. It demanded a generous payment for the flag design. After talking over his request, Congress stated that Mr. Hopkinson was not the *only* person who had worked on designs for the flag. They did not grant him any payment.

4 A Series of Flags

The Declaration of Independence did not end the fighting between England and the colonies. For seven more years, the battles continued.

Most of the colonists used a flag with white stars on a canton of blue. They continued to show the 13 colonies with red and white stripes. But there was no law that said that this was really the American flag.

Finally, on June 14, 1777, the Continental Congress passed a law. It was written to describe the country's flag. Here are the words the colonists used.

. . . that the flag of the thirteen United States be thirteen stripes alternate red and white; that the union be thirteen stars, white in a blue field, representing a new constellation.

The new flag law was a popular idea. The men who passed it in the Continental Congress thought they had described the flag in a way that could not be confused. But they were wrong.

The law did not say how big the canton should be. It did not say how the stars were to be arranged on the blue field. And it did not say how wide the 13 red and white stripes should be.

Some of those who made flags put the stars in rows. Some put them in a circle of 13. Others made a circle of 12 stars with one in the middle.

No one could agree on how many points the stars should have. As more flags were raised throughout the colonies, the number of points ranged from four to eight.

Just two months after the law was passed, a new American flag went into battle at Bennington, Vermont. It was the first flag to lead American armed forces on land.

And what did this Bennington flag look like? It had 13 stripes. But it did not have red ones at the top and bottom, as we see today. There were seven white stripes and six red ones. The top and bottom stripes were white!

On the canton, 11 stars formed an arch. Two other stars were in the corners of the canton. And inside the arch was the number 76. It was a fine flag, and the patriots were glad to carry it.

Bennington flag

This Bennington flag followed all the rules of the flag law, as did many others. But the flags were not all the same.

Adding to the flag confusion were paintings of battles between patriots and the British. Since there were no photographs in those days, a record of a battle had to be painted by hand. If the artist couldn't find a flag at the battle site, he often painted one into the scene. Unfortunately, what the artist painted was often not the flag that had flown over the battlefield. It was what the artist *thought* it should be.

Confusion about the exact design and size of the flag continued. It was 17 years before Congress again described the American flag.

The Continental Congress of 1777 did not leave a written record of *why* it chose the colors red, white, and blue. But five years later, in 1782, those same colors were chosen for the Great Seal of the United States. At that time, Congress stated that red was for heartiness and courage. White was for purity and innocence. And blue was for vigilance, perseverance, and justice.

Great Seal

5 Other Nations Take Note

When a new country forms, it is important that other nations recognize that country. In the 1700s, this was especially important at sea. A captain coming close to a strange ship looked at its flag. Recognizing the flag told him whether to go closer, fight, or run away. If the flag was from a friendly country, a salute was exchanged. The first captain fired his ship's guns into the air. The other ship then fired its guns in reply.

In November 1776, America's flag had received its first foreign salute. The American warship *Andrew Doria* approached Fort Orange on the Dutch West Indies island of St. Eustacia. From the masthead of the *Andrew Doria* flew the Grand Union flag.

The American crew fired a salute in greeting. The men in the fort then answered by firing 11 guns to honor the American flag and the states it represented.

Three months later, on February 14, 1778, the Stars and Stripes flew over Captain John Paul Jones's American ship, *Ranger*, as it passed through Quiberon Bay, France. Jones proudly watched as the French fleet gave a salute of nine guns.

France was an important and powerful country. This salute at Quiberon Bay was formal recognition of the American flag.

In modern times, a ship from a country recognized by the United States may dip its flag to salute a U.S. ship. That is, the flag is lowered slightly, then raised again. The American naval vessel returns the salute by dipping its flag. It is no longer customary to fire guns to salute another nation's flag.

In Battle

In 1779, Captain John Paul Jones sailed across the ocean to chase British ships. The leaders of the American navy heard stories of his brave sea battles.

Jones became such a hero that the United States government gave him a small fleet to take into battle. Captain Jones chose to direct this group of warships from his flagship, the *Bonhomme Richard*. The ship was quite old, but it had 40 guns.

By now, Captain Jones was fighting under another design of the American flag. The flag on the *Bonhomme Richard* had red and white stripes. But it had some blue stripes too. And its stars each had eight points. They were on a very small canton of blue.

John Paul Jones

One night, in English waters, the *Bonhomme Richard* came near an enemy ship, the

Bonhomme Richard and Serapis

Serapis. The English ship was huge. It had 50 guns, all of them pointed at the *Bonhomme Richard*.

23

In the sea battle that followed, guns roared. Smoke filled the air. A cannonball struck the *Bonhomme Richard*. Then another. In the confusion, the American flag was knocked from its mast.

Captain Jones thought of a way to win the battle. Sailing the *Bonhomme Richard* close behind the *Serapis*, Jones ordered his men to rope the two ships together. Soon the American ship was tied to the **stern** of the *Serapis*. The English ship could not turn its guns to aim at the damaged *Bonhomme Richard*.

The English captain saw there was no flag on the American ship. He thought it had been taken down as a signal of **surrender**. He shouted across the water to Jones. Was the American ready to give up?

It was then that John Paul Jones gave his famous answer, "I have not yet begun to fight!" Hearing his proud words, Jones's crew wanted even more to win. At the captain's order, the Americans jumped onto the battleship.

Battling bravely, they went on to win against the larger ship. John Paul Jones signaled victory. Quickly he raised the tattered American flag over the *Serapis*.

In Peacetime

When the war for freedom from England was over, the army of the new United States was very small. The country had only one warship left, and it was soon sold by Congress. From then until a new navy was formed in 1794, only American **merchant ships** carried the Stars and Stripes to foreign ports.

In 1787, a merchant ship, *Columbia*, sailed out of Boston. From its mast flew the American flag. In 1790, the ship returned. It had carried the Stars and Stripes around the world.

The Flag Grows Larger 6

In 1791, Vermont joined the United States. And in 1792, Kentucky was admitted too. After this happened, a flag of 13 stripes and 13 stars no longer represented all the states.

On January 13, 1794, the members of Congress passed a second flag resolution. It was short and, like the first one, not completely clear. Beginning on May 1, 1795, it said, the flag would be "15 stripes, alternate red and white." It was to have a canton with "15 stars, white in a blue field."

Congress did not spend much time on this flag resolution. The United States was a struggling nation. In 1794, it no longer had a navy. Its small army was busy with Indian wars. As before, the representatives in Congress had more urgent matters to discuss.

During 1804 and 1805, explorers Meriwether Lewis and William Clark led an expedition from the Mississippi River to the Pacific Coast of North America, to a spot that is now the state of Washington. They carried with them the 15-stripe flag described by Congress in 1794.

7 War Comes Again

Trouble with England was again brewing. By 1812, a new war had broken out. It was a war about freedom of the seas.

The United States did not seem ready for such a war. England had an army and more than 100 battleships. The United States Navy had not a single ship that large. It had only a few **frigates** and **sloops**. In all, the American ships carried only 412 guns. The British navy had 10 times that many.

But the British had not counted on the bravery and daring of the American captains. During the next two years, the small fleet turned in victory after victory.

There were some defeats too. One of the worst was the loss of the American ship *Chesapeake* in the waters near Boston. In the battle, her injured captain, James Lawrence, uttered the famous words, "Don't give up the ship." Within a few minutes, he was dead.

Three months later, to honor the loss of Lawrence and his crew, Commander Oliver H. Perry raised a special flag over his flagship, the *Lawrence*. The flag's field was blue. In white letters it proclaimed the dead captain's order, "Don't Give Up the Ship." With these words flying from his mast, Perry went on to defeat the British navy at Lake Erie.

Oliver H. Perry

Commodore Perry and Battle of Lake Erie

When Perry wrote his report of the Lake Erie battle, he used other words that have gone down in American naval history. "We have met the enemy and they are ours."

But the British continued to fight. In 1814, they marched into Washington, D.C. There they burned the Capitol Building and many other government offices.

A City in Danger

The British seemed to be headed for Baltimore, Maryland. Fort McHenry, in the city's harbor, was Baltimore's hope of defense. It must be prepared for war.

Major George Armistead wanted Fort McHenry's flag to be large enough "that the British will have no difficulty seeing it from a distance." He sent Commodore Joshua Barney and General John Stricker to the home of Baltimore's best seamstress, Mary Pickersgill.

The two men described for Mrs. Pickersgill what they needed. The flag, with its 15 stars and 15 stripes, must be of strong woolen fabric. And it must be larger than any flag made before. The **banner** was to be 30 feet by 42 feet.

Think of 30 feet as being the height of a three-story building. That gives some idea of how very large this flag was to be.

Mary Pickersgill

To have the space needed to spread out their sewing, Mary Pickersgill and her daughter, Caroline, moved their woolen

cloth, needles, and thread to the second floor of an old
distillery. Kneeling there, by candlelight, they bent over their
hurried task.

When the flag was
finished, Mrs. Pickersgill
was paid $405.90—a great
deal of money in those days.

The flag was taken to
Fort McHenry to be raised.
It weighed 90 pounds. The
weight was a problem.
Would the flagpole be
strong enough? It would
have to bear the weight of
a 90-pound flag whipping
in the wind.

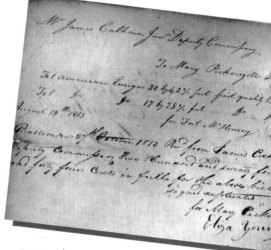

The men at Fort McHenry
dug a hole 9 feet deep. At the
bottom, they nailed together two

Original payment receipt
for the creation of the flag

heavy wooden cross beams in the form of an X. Where the
beams crossed, a strong wooden pole was attached. It rose
straight upward, high above the top of the hole.

The 9 feet of soil was replaced and packed down. This
allowed the pole to remain upright, holding the flag aloft. The
plan worked well, except for very windy days. Then the heavy
flag had to be taken down and replaced with a smaller one.

Today, the original flag made by Mary
Pickersgill can be seen at the Smithsonian
Institution in Washington, D.C. But it no longer
measures 30 feet by 42 feet. The woolen fabric
was damaged by years of moisture and
handling. Pieces **frayed** and fell off. Now its
size is just 28 feet by 32 feet.

8 The National Anthem

As military leaders in Baltimore had feared, the British arrived to attack their city. British warships sailed closer and closer to Fort McHenry. Their ships fired guns and rockets at the fort with its huge flag.

The fort's guns boomed. The British fired back. Smoke filled the air. The brave Americans fighting there could see their flag above it all.

On a ship far down the bay stood an American lawyer and poet named Francis Scott Key. He hoped those fighting at the fort could save it from the British. All night long, he watched the battle.

And why was Francis Scott Key in Baltimore's harbor? A week before, he had set out to meet with officials of the British fleet. Key was the lawyer for Dr. William Beanes, who had been arrested by the British at a battle near Washington, D.C.

Key arrived at Baltimore a few days before the British attack upon Fort McHenry. He and an American colonel talked with the British on a **truce** ship. Dr. Beanes was on the ship too. Key bargained with the British officers. An offer of money was probably made. At last, the British agreed to let Dr. Beanes go free.

By the time Key had arranged for Dr. Beanes' freedom, he had been with the British for many hours. He knew how many ships they had. And he knew where those ships were. He may even have known what time the attack would start. The British could not let him go ashore to tell what he knew.

Key was not a prisoner. Neither was the American colonel who had come with him. And soon, Dr. Beanes was free also. But the three Americans could not leave the ship until after the battle had ended.

On September 13, 1814, Francis Scott Key, the colonel, and Dr. Beanes stood on the deck of the British warship. Night began to fall. Key watched the flag until it was too dark to see. All night, his eyes searched for some sight of it.

Sometimes, when the British shot off a rocket, the sky lit up. Yes, yes, there it was! Key could still see the flag in the rocket's glare.

Morning came. It was September 14. The sky grew lighter. Key stared through the hazy dawn toward Fort McHenry.

There it was! The flag was still there. The British ships were moving away from the fight. The brave men at Fort McHenry had saved Baltimore!

Francis Scott Key was proud to be an American. He wanted to write down how he felt. So he wrote a poem about what he had seen that morning.

Later, Key's poem was set to music. And in 1931, it became America's national anthem.

O say, can you see,
By the dawn's early light,
What so proudly we hailed,
At the twilight's last gleaming . .

Today, we proudly sing Francis Scott Key's words at meetings, sports events, and parades.

31

9 More Changes for the Country's Flag

Soon after the War of 1812, it became clear that adding a star and stripe for each new state would not be wise. Five more states had joined the union. Now there were 20. How could a flag be large enough to represent each one? The idea seemed impossible.

Peter Wendover, a congressman from New York State, hoped to solve this problem. He spoke to members of Congress. "It is time for a new flag law," he told them. "And I am willing to work for it." He asked his fellow congressmen to appoint him chairman of a special flag committee.

For advice, Peter Wendover turned to Captain Samuel Reid, a naval hero from the War of 1812. Reid had been urging the navy to do something about ordering a flag that everyone could recognize.

When he met with Wendover, Reid suggested reducing the number of stripes from 15 to 13, one for each of the original states. This plan would help lookouts on the navy's ships to identify their fellow Americans.

Samuel Reid

Reid feared that if more and more stripes were added, each stripe would become thinner. If this happened, it would be hard to identify the flag on a ship far out at sea.

Wendover's committee met many times. He pointed out to the members that many different flags flew right there in Washington. At that very moment, above them on the

Capitol building, was a flag with 13 stars and 13 stripes. Flying over other public buildings in Washington at the same time were a least three other designs. The number of stripes varied from 9 to 18.

The committee continued to work slowly. Wendover could not make them hurry. Meanwhile, Tennessee, Ohio, Louisiana, Indiana, and Mississippi had been granted stars on the flag. A new design was needed even more!

A New Flag Law

Early in 1818, after months of discussion, Congress passed a flag bill that was signed into law by President James Monroe. The bill stated that after July 4 of that year, the American flag would show 13 stripes and 20 stars.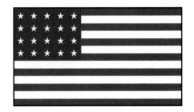

And in the future, a new star would be added for each state admitted to the U.S. The number of stripes would always be 13.

Each time a state was added, its new star would appear the following Fourth of July. In that way, the admission of new states would celebrate the birthday of the United States.

Captain Reid was pleased with what Congress had decided. In a hurry to put the law into use, Reid asked his wife to make the first flag of 13 stripes and 20 stars. She began sewing that very day. And she did not ask Congress to pay her for her work.

But the confusion was not over. The new flag law did not say how the stars were to be arranged. Mrs. Reid sewed them into one huge **composite** star made up of 20 much smaller stars. Her flag was raised over the Capitol dome on April 13, 1818.

Congressman Wendover had hoped the new law would say how the stars were to be arranged. But other representatives in Congress wanted that decision left open. More confusion resulted as more 13-stripe, 20-star flags were completed.

Later in 1818, President Monroe issued a presidential **proclamation** saying that the stars should be arranged in four equal, **parallel** rows of five each. And that another star was to be added whenever a new state was admitted.

Still no law about the placement of the stars on the United States flag has been passed. When a state is added, the new arrangement is again decided by presidential proclamation.

James Monroe

Slave or Free?

In the three years following the 1818 flag law, four more stars were added. They stood for Illinois, Alabama, Maine, and Missouri.

But adding each of these states caused arguments in Congress. The Northern states and the Southern states could not agree about slavery. While some people in all parts of the country owned slaves, most of them were in the South.

Each time a new state was considered, arguments broke out about whether that state's blacks would be slaves or free men and women. Below is a chart that shows the way those arguments ended and the dates when each new star appeared.

Illinois	July 4, 1818	21st star	free
Alabama	July 4, 1810	22nd star	slave
Maine	July 4, 1820	23rd star	free
Missouri	July 4, 1822	24th star	slave

For the next 14 years, no new states were added. The American flag continued to show 24 stars.

A New Name for the Flag

On March 17, 1824, friends surprised 21-year-old William Driver with a special birthday present. Driver, who lived in Salem, Massachusetts, would soon have his dreams come true. All his life he had wanted to become a sailor.

Knowing that each ship needed a flag, Driver's mother and a group of friends had carefully sewn a large American flag for him. When William Driver opened the package, his eyes grew wide. There was no gift he would have liked better. Proud of his new banner, he declared, "I'll call her Old Glory. That's right, Old Glory."

From that day on, William Driver took Old Glory along whenever he went to sea. Serving on ships that sailed around the world, he advanced in rank. In time, he became Captain Driver. Always, Old Glory flew from his mast.

In 1837, Captain Driver left the sea and settled in Nashville, Tennessee. There he flew Old Glory from his home.

But things changed in 1861 when the Civil War began. Tennessee seceded from the Union. After that, Driver's neighbors noticed Old Glory had disappeared from in front of his house.

In February of 1862, Union soldiers marched into Nashville and took back the city for the United States. When Driver saw that the Southern soldiers were gone, he ripped open the comforter on his bed. Hidden inside, in place of stuffing, was Old Glory. Driver had carefully hidden it from the enemy.

Driver and his friends hurried to the state capitol building. Climbing to the top of the dome, William Driver once more raised his beloved flag, saying, "Thank God. I lived to raise Old Glory on the dome of the capitol of Tennessee."

Today, William Driver's Old Glory is on display at the Smithsonian Institution in Washington, D.C.

10 The Stars and Stripes Meet a Powerful Friend

Millard Fillmore

Between 1836 and 1851, seven more territories joined the United States. They were Arkansas, Michigan, Florida, Texas, Iowa, Wisconsin, and California. Now the flag had 31 stars. There were still arguments about slavery, but this period was marked by more peace than anger in Congress.

America was at peace with other nations too. President Millard Fillmore and the members of Congress turned their attention to building goodwill with other countries.

President Fillmore hoped Americans could trade with the people of Japan. Selling goods between the two countries would earn more money for both Japanese and American merchants.

But there was a problem. The Japanese **emperor** would not agree to let ships of other nations enter his country's waters. In those days, there were no radios, no telephones, and no TVs. Trade talks could only be held face to face.

President Fillmore turned to a naval officer he trusted. That man was Matthew C. Perry, younger brother of Oliver Perry, a hero in the War of 1812.

Matthew Perry had shown his own military talent in the short war between the U.S. and Mexico in 1847. The navy offered Perry a small fleet of ships. Could he get into Edo Harbor?

Perry studied everything he could find about Japan. Then he filled the holds of his ships with presents for the emperor—farm tools, a telescope, whiskey, books, and rifles. Along with these was a new invention he knew the emperor would like. It was a tiny toy train that pulled a passenger car along its tracks.

Bravely, Perry sailed into Edo Harbor on July 8, 1853. His flagship, the *Mississippi*, led the way. The American flag, with its 31 stars, flew from the mast of each American vessel. Perry wanted to impress the Japanese with the power of the United States.

Commodore
Matthew Perry

The city of Edo, Japan, would later be renamed Tokyo.

JAPAN

PACIFIC OCEAN

Edo (renamed Tokyo)
Edo Harbor

37

Past the smaller ships of Japan, the Americans sailed. Some of the Japanese sailors tried to jump onto the American ships, but the American sailors pushed them off.

Perry led his small fleet forward, past the emperor's navy and hundreds of small fishing vessels.

Docking at the capital, Perry presented a trade proposal to the Japanese. It contained rules that would benefit both countries. But the Japanese would not agree. They did not make Perry welcome in their country.

The Americans sailed away for a seven-month visit to China. The Japanese emperor had plenty of time to think about trade.

When Perry returned with seven American ships on February 13, 1854, the Japanese were again impressed with the power shown by the U.S. Navy.

Now the emperor was ready to sign a treaty of trade and friendship with the United States. The treaty also included an agreement that American sailors would be well treated when they came to Japan.

Perry had handled his assignment well. And the American flag had become known and respected in the Orient.

The War Between the States 11

During the next five years, two more states, Minnesota and Oregon, were admitted. Now the American flag showed 33 stars. But again the issue of slavery grew more heated. For months, Congress debated the fate of Kansas. Finally, that state's admission was approved.

But before the new flag showing 34 stars could be raised on July 4, 1861, war broke out.

In 1860, the Republican Party had chosen Abraham Lincoln as its candidate for president. The Republican Party was against slavery.

When Lincoln was elected, leaders of the Southern states were angry. They feared the country's Northern states would have enough votes in Congress to end slavery. Southern plantation owners insisted they could not grow their crops without slaves to work in the fields. More and more, Southerners in Congress spoke of leaving the United States.

Abraham Lincoln

The nation was hopelessly divided. Then on December 20, 1860, South Carolina seceded from the Union. A month later, six more Southern states also left. Later, four more would join them.

Bombing Fort Sumter

The leaders of South Carolina were angry. Fort Sumter, a U.S. military post, was in their state. It lay right on the shore of the harbor in the city of Charleston.

The citizens were furious. "Charleston is a Southern city," they shouted. "The Northerners must be driven away!"

On April 12, 1861, Southern soldiers fired upon the U.S. troops at Fort Sumter. For 34 hours, the South **bombarded** the fort.

U.S. Major General Robert Anderson was in command of Fort Sumter. He saw that unless he surrendered, many lives would be lost. Anderson hauled down the Stars and Stripes. As quickly as possible, his men climbed onto U.S. Navy vessels. The ships headed northward, leaving Fort Sumter to the Southern troops.

Losing the battle at Fort Sumter upset and saddened many Americans. But at least no one had been killed. War was a terrible thing! The next time shots were fired, would Americans be killing Americans?

After Fort Sumter, there were many in Congress who wanted to change the American flag. They wanted to take away

A respected American joined in the discussion of whether the seceded states should still be represented on the American flag. Samuel F. B. Morse, well-known for his invention of the telegraph, suggested that the Stars and Stripes be divided into two flags. In his plan, the canton would be cut diagonally from top to bottom. The North would retain 23 stars and the upper six and one-half stripes. The 11 stars below the diagonal and the other six and one-half stripes would go to the South. Both flags would have white cloth added to bring them back to a rectangular shape.

Samuel F. B. Morse

Neither President Lincoln nor the Congress gave this unusual suggestion much thought.

the stars that represented the 11 states that had seceded. But President Lincoln said "No!" He wanted the Southern states to be able to change their minds and come back. He wanted the country united again.

The war that began at Fort Sumter divided Americans against other Americans. And it lasted for four bitter years. Sadly, before the fighting ended, thousands of Americans, young and old, would die.

The Confederacy and Its Flags

The 11 Southern states that seceded banded together. Those states were Alabama, Arkansas, Florida, Georgia, Louisiana, Mississippi, North Carolina, South Carolina, Tennessee, Texas, and Virginia. They called their new nation the Confederate States of America.

The man chosen to lead the Confederate States as their president was Jefferson Davis. Davis had served as a U.S. senator and as Secretary of War in President Franklin Pierce's **cabinet**.

The new Confederate States of America needed a flag. The first one was adopted on March 4, 1861. It was called the Stars and Bars. It had only three stripes—two broad red ones with a white stripe in the middle. The canton was blue. It had seven white stars in a circle. These stood for the seven states that had first left the United States.

Stars and Bars

But there was a problem with the Stars and Bars. An early battle between the North and South happened at a place in Virginia called Bull Run. During the fighting, gun smoke filled the air. It partly hid the flags of both sides.

The two flags, each red and white with a blue canton, were hard to tell apart. Soldiers were not sure who was on their side and who was an enemy. The Stars and Bars would not do as a Southern flag!

So in July of 1861, the South made a special Confederate battle flag. Its field was red. Across the field ran two blue and white stripes in the shape of an X. There were 13 stars on the X.

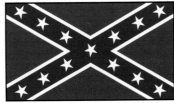

Confederate flag

At the time the flag was designed, only 11 Confederate states had seceded, but they hoped at least two others would soon join them.

The battle flag was never an official national flag of the Confederacy. But it was popular with the fighting men from the South.

Today, if you look at the state flags of Mississippi and Georgia, you can see part of the Confederate battle flag included in each design.

Later, there was a second national flag. It was adopted in May of 1863. The field of this flag was white. The red, white, and blue battle flag was shown in the corner and served as the flag's canton.

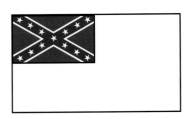

This new flag went into battle. But it, too, caused confusion. If there was not much wind, the flag hung limply from its pole. When that happened, only the large white field showed. It looked like a flag of surrender! The enemy might think the South's men were giving up.

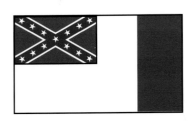

The Confederates decided to add a broad vertical stripe of red to the end of the white field. This new design was adopted by the Confederate States of America in February of 1865. By then, the War Between the States was almost over.

A Woman of Courage

One of the most famous and best-loved stories of the Civil War is that of 97-year-old Barbara Frietchie. Mrs. Frietchie was loyal to the Union. She was sad when the Southern states seceded.

In 1862, when Confederate troops marched into Barbara Frietchie's town of Frederick, Maryland, her neighbors hid their American flags. They did not want to get into trouble with the Southerners. But Barbara Frietchie did not take Old Glory down. And she did not hide it in a comforter as William Driver had done in Tennessee.

No, Barbara Frietchie was brave. She hung her flag right out on the front of her house. There it waved in front of Confederate General Stonewall Jackson and his men. The men were angry to see Old Glory there.

Some of them complained to General Jackson. But, seeing the brave old woman at her window, Jackson ordered his men to leave her in safety.

In 1863, the poet John Greenleaf Whittier wrote a poem about Barbara Frietchie's bravery for the magazine *Atlantic Monthly*.

"Shoot, if you must this old gray head,
But spare your country's flag," she said.

According to the poem, General Jackson's answer was

"Who touches a hair of yon gray head
Dies like a dog! March on!" he said.

If you go to Mount Olivette Cemetery in Frederick, Maryland, you will find the graves of both Barbara Frietchie and Francis Scott Key.

War's End

In 1865, the war was over at last. The South was again part of the United States. During the fighting, two states, Kansas and West Virginia, had joined the Union. Now there were 35 stars on the U.S. flag.

On October 31, 1864, Nevada had also been approved for statehood. On the next Fourth of July, its star would appear.

On April 14, 1865, five days after General Robert E. Lee surrendered the Confederate forces at Appomattox Court House, Virginia, the American flag was again raised over Fort Sumter. Once more, General Robert Anderson was in charge. The flag-raising was accompanied by a 100-gun salute.

But that historic occasion was hardly noticed by the public. Something else had happened that left the nation shocked.

President Lincoln was dead of a gunshot wound.

13 The Nation Is Again United

After the Civil War, Americans turned their attention to what many called the Wild West. This huge area spread from the Missouri River to the Pacific Ocean. Settlers had been going there since the early 1800s. Now still more Americans were ready to make a move.

Stories about the territories excited young families. Farmers and miners hurried west to seek their

Wagon trains moving west

fortunes. The population grew in the new lands. Many who traveled there hoped to form new states.

Nebraska's star appeared on the flag in 1867, largely because of the rush of new settlers. Colorado, in 1876, had a special distinction. It was called the "Centennial State" because its star celebrated the 100th birthday of the nation. Now the blue canton showed 38 stars.

Two Special Days for the Flag

On May 30, 1868, the United States observed a new national holiday—a day on which the Stars and Stripes would be proudly flown. The holiday was called Decoration Day, because it was a special time when Americans placed flowers and small flags on the graves of those who died in the Civil War.

Today, Decoration Day is called Memorial Day by most Americans, and it reminds us of all Americans who have died in wars.

★　★　★　★　★

The holiday we know as Flag Day began slowly.

Records show it was first observed in Connecticut on June 14, 1861. The idea for this onetime event had been suggested in the newspaper *The Hartford Courant*.

In 1877, the holiday was first observed nationwide. To celebrate the 100th anniversary of the adoption of the Stars and Stripes by the Continental Congress, the U.S. government asked that all public buildings fly the flag on June 14. Again, Flag Day was a special one-day event.

Then in 1885, a Wisconsin teacher named B. J. Cigrand wanted to honor the Stars and Stripes. He planned a special event for his students and called it "Flag Birthday." The event was held on June 14, the 108th anniversary of the adoption of the Stars and Stripes by the Continental Congress. Each June, Cigrand interested more Wisconsin teachers in the idea of such a "Flag Birthday" or "Flag Day."

The idea of Flag Day grew slowly. Each year, a few more American schools and cities joined in. Finally, on May 30, 1916, President Woodrow Wilson announced that June 14th would become a holiday each year. It would honor Old Glory with patriotic exercises all over the United States.

Today on Flag Day, Americans hang flags on homes, businesses, and public buildings. Civic groups often hold community parades.

Most schools hold special programs. Students recite the Pledge of Allegiance. They talk about the early days of the United States and sing "The Star-Spangled Banner."

More Stars Are Added 14

The West continued to grow. In 1880, the first railroad across the U.S. was completed. It opened up land to still more settlers.

By 1889, many more states were seeking admission to the U.S. In the eight months between November 1889 and July 1890, Congress voted in favor of North Dakota, South Dakota, Montana, Washington, and Idaho. These actions meant all five new states would gain their stars on July 4, 1890. Only once before had so many new stars been added to Old Glory since the original 13 colonies declared their independence. And the addition of Wyoming was still under discussion.

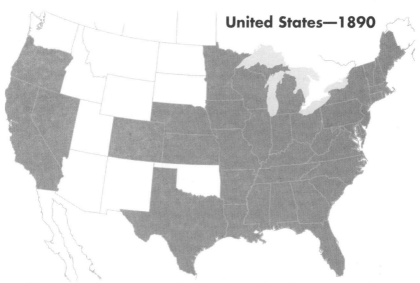

United States—1890

But again there was confusion about the placement and number of stars in Old Glory's canton. Some flag makers made banners that added five new stars, but not one for Wyoming. Others decided to add Wyoming, believing its star would soon be needed.

For a year, various flags flew. Some had 43 stars. A few showed 44, the correct number after Wyoming was admitted in 1891. Still other flag companies placed 45 stars upon the canton, hoping to stay ahead of the need for a new flag.

In 1887, President Grover Cleveland ordered that all battle flags captured during the Civil War be returned to the South. This idea threw Congress and the public into a **frenzy**. Representatives in Congress and citizens in the streets argued loudly. Some agreed with the president. Others wanted the flags burned. They said the South should give up its battle flags forever.

Grover Cleveland

After a week of near riots, President Cleveland revoked his order.

In 1905, at a time when Congress was less divided, President Theodore Roosevelt ordered the rebel flags returned. The Civil War had been over for 40 years. This time there was no protest against the president's plan.

The Pledge to the Flag 15

In 1892, President Benjamin Harrison called for patriotic ceremonies in all American schools. This was to honor the 400th anniversary of America's discovery.

Francis Bellamy was a magazine editor from Boston. He worked for *The Youth's Companion*. Bellamy and another patriot, James B. Upham, wrote a Pledge of Allegiance to the American flag. It was shorter than the one we use now. Bellamy published it in his magazine.

Millions of school children in the United States repeated the pledge in their patriotic ceremonies on October 21, 1892. In 1923 and again in 1924, the American Legion added words to what Bellamy had written.

In 1942, Congress made the Pledge of Allegiance part of its code for the proper use of Old Glory. And in 1954, it added the words "under God."

The familiar pledge now reads

I pledge allegiance to the flag of the United States of America and to the Republic for which it stands, one Nation, under God, indivisible, with liberty and justice for all.

16 America as a World Power

In 1898, the United States had been at peace for 33 years. Two years before, Utah had been admitted to the U.S. The stars on Old Glory's canton numbered 45.

But all was not quiet in the nearby Caribbean Sea. Trouble was brewing on the island of Cuba, south of Florida. On February 15, the U.S. battleship *Maine* exploded in the Cuban harbor of Havana. The blast killed 260 Americans—two navy officers and 258 enlisted men.

Spain controlled Cuba. Had the Spanish dared to blow up the *Maine*?

Americans were shocked. And they were angry. Worries arose about Cuba. Some U.S. citizens had relatives there. The Cuban people had been in danger for years while the island struggled to break free from Spanish rule.

The American public was furious with the Spanish government. The cry "Remember the Maine!" echoed through the nation. On April 25, 1898, the U.S. Congress declared war against Spain—a war to be fought under the 45-star flag.

Theodore Roosevelt, the U.S. Secretary of the Navy, resigned from the president's cabinet. For him, it was more important to fight the Spanish. He led a band of Americans he called the Rough Riders. Roosevelt and his fighting men were heroes in battle.

A few years later, in 1901, Theodore Roosevelt became the 26th president of the United States.

Theodore Roosevelt

52

The Spanish American War ended 114 days after it began. Most fighting had been limited to Cuba, but there were also battles at Manila Bay in the Philippine Islands.

Spain had lost the war. In peace talks, its government agreed to give up several properties. Cuba would become a free country. The United States would own Puerto Rico, the Philippines, and the Pacific Ocean island of Guam.

With these new territories, the Stars and Stripes became a flag flown around the world. The United States was now a world power. To show its might, a fleet of 16 U.S. battleships sailed around the world between 1907–1909. The American flag proudly waved from each mast.

On July 4, 1908, another star was added. For many years an area, which the Choctaw tribe called the "Land of the Red People," had been set aside for the use of American Indians. In 1889, Congress opened this land to all interested settlers. Thousands of families—white, African American, and Indian— poured into the territory. After many months of discussion in Congress, these lands became the state of Oklahoma. Old Glory now had 46 stars in her canton.

17 In Quest of the Poles

Population in the United States continued to grow. Few areas between the Atlantic and Pacific Oceans remained that had not already become states.

The U.S. territories of Puerto Rico, Guam, and the Philippine Islands flew the Stars and Stripes. But another search was under way—an exploration northward.

Robert Peary's Long Effort

For 15 years, U.S. Navy engineer Robert E. Peary had devoted all his spare time to finding the exact point of the North Pole. With all his energies, he longed to someday reach that spot.

Using any vacation time he could get from the navy, Peary put together one discovery team after another. When his navy superiors limited his time away from his duties, Peary asked for help from President Theodore Roosevelt. The president, who also loved outdoor exploring, ordered that Peary should have the time off he needed. So Peary took a five-year leave of absence from the navy.

By 1909, Peary had made six expeditions, each time coming closer to the North Pole. Americans began to know his name and what he wanted to do.

Peary had learned many things during his trips into the cold and danger of the Arctic. On his early trips, he had taken strong, muscular American men who could lift heavy loads. But as the years went by, Peary chose others who were small and **wiry** in build. This gave more room for supplies in the **sledges**. And it lightened the loads pulled by his dog teams.

Every year, he designed new sledges. He wanted them to be faster and to float where that was needed.

Peary got closer and closer to the North Pole each year. And he had something special under his thick clothes. It was a silk flag, made for him by his wife.

Peary wanted to leave his flag at the North Pole. But on every trip, he had met troubles that forced him to turn back. Each time, he carefully cut off a piece of the flag and left it at the farthest point north he had reached.

The Eskimos of the Arctic lands were necessary to Peary's plans. Each spring, they greeted him with cheers as his new exploration began. Some of them had been working with Peary since he first began exploring the Arctic.

The Eskimos taught the Americans how to build igloos, the best shelters for nights that reached 50 degrees below zero. And an igloo could be used over and over, not like a tent that had to be put up and taken down.

Admiral Robert Peary with his huskies

The Eskimos showed the Americans how to recognize ice that was too thin to support their weight. Just as important, they helped hunt and prepare Arctic animals like seals and musk oxen to add some fresh meat to the adventurers' diet.

On his final trip to the North Pole in 1909, Peary had 6 American assistants and 17 Eskimos. In all, 19 sledges, pulled by 133 dogs, would carry this group and its supplies.

Along with canned fruits and vegetables, milk, tea, and alcohol, Peary took huge supplies of pemmican. This is lean meat, dried and pounded until it is very thin. Raisins and sugar were sometimes added for quick energy.

Before a trip, Peary had huge supplies of pemmican prepared. There were 500-pound red tins of pemmican to feed the dogs. These were stored low on the sledges. Tins of pemmican for humans were blue and weighed 50 pounds.

To begin the exploration, Peary's ship, the *Roosevelt*, took the men as far north as any ship could go. From there, they faced life in the bitter cold, open air.

Commander Peary divided his men and dogs into six teams. The team **breaking trail** at the front of the line had the hardest job. When they became tired and stiff with cold, those men returned to the igloos at base camp. After a short rest, they loaded more supplies on their sledges and brought them forward. In this way, like a relay race, the 1909 expedition made its way toward the North Pole.

When his compass showed he was only 133 miles from the North Pole, Commander Peary began to send some of the teams and their sledges back to the *Roosevelt*.

He chose the strongest men and dogs to stay with him for the final effort. Now there were five sledges, pulled by 40 dogs. The men in Peary's final team were his trusted African American assistant, Matthew Henson, and four Eskimos of the Inuit tribe.

For five days, the final team struggled north, often forced to stop for hours when they came to open water too wide to cross. This meant waiting for the ice to freeze again. Finally the expedition reached a point just three miles from the North Pole.

Peary fell, exhausted. He could go no farther. But, the next day, he pushed on. He crossed the spot his compass told him was the North Pole. Then he crossed it over and over to be sure he had been successful. Taking out his camera, he photographed the view southward from every angle.

Few people knew about the flag Commander Peary carried under his layers of warm clothing. It had been with him on each of his seven expeditions. At last he could place it at the Pole.

Peary took out his American flag. Its canton showed 46 stars. On April 6, 1909, Commander Peary declared, "This is the last and most northerly camp on the earth." To honor his triumph for America, Peary placed the remainder of the silk flag into a hollow in a mound of ice.

When Peary returned home, he learned that another explorer, Frederick Cook, was claiming to have reached the North Pole ahead of him. Peary was puzzled and sad. The public did not give him the welcome he had expected.

Later, Cook's claims were shown to be false. Robert Peary was at last given credit for planting Old Glory at the North Pole.

The Flights of Admiral Richard E. Byrd

About 20 years after Robert Peary raised Old Glory at the North Pole, another American explorer appeared. He was Admiral Richard E. Byrd. On May 9, 1926, Byrd became the first man to fly over the North Pole in an airplane.

In 1929, Byrd and his chief pilot flew to the South Pole. There they raised the Stars and Stripes over an Antarctic base they named Little America.

Byrd made a second flight over the South Pole in 1947. He was the first man to fly an airplane over both poles.

Richard E. Byrd in Antarctica

From Sea to Shining Sea 18

On July 4, 1912, two new stars were added to the American flag. Arizona and New Mexico had become states.

Now all the land from the Atlantic Ocean to the Pacific Ocean and all the land from the Canadian border to the Mexican border had become states in the United States.

The new flag, with its 48 stars, would become America's flag for the longest period without change. Under that flag, the United States grew into an even more important world power.

But like the rest of the world, the United States would face challenges. In 1914, much of Europe was involved in a major war, later called World War I. While Americans did not fight in this war until 1917, it caused great changes in American life. And, when Americans went to Europe to fight in the war, the 48-star flag waved above them.

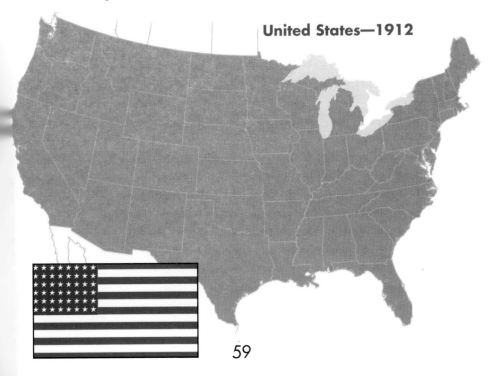

United States—1912

19 A Mountain Called Suribachi

America did not join World War II by choice.

Japanese forces attacked Pearl Harbor on December 7, 1941. Suddenly, the United States was at war. The 48-star flag flew from army posts and navy ships all over the world. It was painted on the sides of American airplanes. And it was proudly flown by citizens at home.

In February 1945, Marines fighting in the Pacific faced a fierce battle over a small island. It was called Iwo Jima. The island was 760 miles south of Japan. America and her allies needed it for an airfield to send bombers over Tokyo, Japan's capital.

The island was full of caves. In those caves, 21,000 Japanese soldiers hid. They were there to keep the Americans and their allies away.

Iwo Jima was a flat, ugly island shaped like a pork chop. On the widest part of the pork chop rose a steep mountain. The mountain's name was Suribachi.

On February 19, 1945, U.S. Marines landed on the narrow part of the island and pushed their way toward the mountain. Three days of bloody fighting followed. Marines crawled up Mount Suribachi on their stomachs as bullets whistled over their heads. They gained just inches at a time.

Toward evening on February 23, the Marines charged the Japanese at the mountaintop and drove them away. The brave Americans were proud of their victory.

Even before the battle was over, a group of Marines had picked up a length of Japanese water pipe and fastened a small American flag to it. As the fighting stopped, the men prepared to raise the flag.

The flag they had brought was small. It measured only 28 inches by 54 inches. Such a small Stars and Stripes would not be seen from far away. So one of the Marines hurried down a trail to the beach.

He took a flag from one of the American ships. It was one that had flown at Pearl Harbor. This new flag was large and easier to see.

The young Marine stumbled back up Mount Suribachi. His buddies were waiting. They had found a longer piece of pipe to use as a flagpole.

As the smaller flag was lowered, six men got ready to raise the larger one. Three news photographers were nearby. When the flag went up, one of them lifted his camera at just the right time. He snapped a picture that would forever be important to the American people.

The flag-raising photo at Iwo Jima appeared over and over in newspapers and magazines. It was pictured on a postage stamp. And later, it was used as a model for the Marine Corps Memorial at Arlington Cemetery. You can visit the memorial there today—across the Potomac River from Washington, D.C.

The raising of the Stars and Stripes on Mount Suribachi has become one of the great symbols of America and her flag.

The first flag raised on Mount Suribachi can be seen today at the Marine Corps Museum in Quantico, Virginia. The second, and larger, flag flew only three weeks. It was torn apart by the fierce winds on Mount Suribachi.

20 New States Are Again Admitted

In 1959, Alaska's star joined the 48 on the canton of the Stars and Stripes. It had been 47 years since America had welcomed a new state.

This was the first time a state was added that was not within the Continental United States—the area bordered by Canada, Mexico, and the Pacific and Atlantic Oceans. A year later, Hawaii's star was added. Here again, the new state was separated from the others, this time by thousands of miles of ocean.

With its 50 stars, Old Glory had grown and changed, as had the nation.

The Stars and Stripes
on the Moon

On July 20, 1969, Americans gathered around their radios and television sets. Something amazing was about to happen. America was putting men on the moon!

The mission was named Apollo 11. In the spacecraft were three American astronauts, Neil Armstrong, Edwin "Buzz" Aldrin, and Michael Collins. All were experienced at space travel with NASA, the National Aeronautics and Space Administration.

Neil Armstrong was commander of the Apollo 11 flight. One of the first men named as a U.S. astronaut in 1962, he had paved the way for the moon attempt. And, on an earlier flight, he had been the first astronaut to dock two spacecraft together.

Neil Armstrong, Michael Collins, and Edwin (Buzz) Aldrin

Buzz Aldrin and Michael Collins had been named to the team of U.S. astronauts only one year after Armstrong. Now, on Apollo 11, Collins would circle the moon in the **command module**, *Columbia*. That spacecraft was essential for their return to Earth.

Aldrin was to join Neil Armstrong in the smaller **lunar module**, *Eagle*. Those two men would walk upon the moon's surface.

The astronauts separated the *Eagle* from *Columbia*. The *Eagle* drifted slowly to a landing on the moon's surface.

Neil Armstrong paused for a moment, then switched off *Eagle*'s engine. Over his radio, he reported to the space center in Houston, Texas. "The *Eagle* has landed!"

All of America heard the message! The astronauts hurried to raise the Stars and Stripes. They were being watched by the largest television audience in history.

The flag's pole sunk easily into the first few inches of the moon's surface, a fine, grainy powder. Below that, all was hard rock. The pole would go in only a couple of inches. It didn't look very sturdy, but the astronauts had done their best. They stepped back and saluted Old Glory.

The moon has no atmosphere. No breezes blow there. Knowing this, the scientists at NASA had stiffened the flag by sewing a metal wire along its top. This gave the appearance of a flag blowing in the breeze.

After gathering dirt and rocks from the moon's surface, Armstrong and Aldrin prepared to blast off in the lunar module and rejoin Michael Collins in *Columbia*.

As *Eagle* rose from the moon, the two men looked back. To their surprise, they saw the Stars and Stripes flutter. The force from their rocket's exhaust had caused a breeze on the moon.

"That was beautiful," Buzz Aldrin told the waiting world.

The Flag Draws Americans Together 22

On September 11, 2001, terrorists attacked the United States at New York City and Washington, D.C.

Americans watched their television sets in horror. Thousands of their fellow citizens were dying in front of their eyes. Those killed were not in the military. They did not have weapons. They had no way to protect themselves.

The country was in shock. But one symbol seemed to calm people and make them feel united. That symbol was the American flag.

The people of the United States got out their flags. Those who had flown them only on holidays began to raise the Stars and Stripes each morning.

The words of the Pledge of Allegiance had new meaning. "The Star-Spangled Banner" brought tears to many eyes.

In good times and in bad, the American flag deserves our respect, loyalty, and love.

Some Interesting Facts About the American Flag

To correctly show respect to the flag, it should be raised in the morning and taken down at sunset. Flags that fly day and night must be properly lighted in times of darkness. And when the weather is bad enough to damage the fabric, the flag should be taken down.

Old Glory is flown 24 hours a day at all U.S. Customs ports of entry.

In addition, there are eight national sites in the United States that fly the Stars and Stripes day and night. Four of them were designated by presidential proclamation. The others are by tradition.

By presidential proclamation

★ Fort McHenry National Monument, Baltimore, Maryland (since 1948)

★ Flag House Square, Baltimore, the home of Mary Pickersgill (since 1954)

★ Iwo Jima Marine Memorial, Arlington, Virginia (since 1961)

★ The U.S. Capitol, east and west wings (since World War I)

By tradition

★ Over the grave of Francis Scott Key, Frederick, Maryland (since 1916)

★ Worcester War Memorial, Massachusetts (since 1933)

★ The Plaza, Taos, New Mexico (since 1861)

★ Deadwood, South Dakota (since 1941)

Changes in the U.S. Flag Since 1777

New States	Number of Stars	Date Star Appeared
Original Thirteen	13	June 14, 1777
Vermont, Kentucky	15	May 1, 1795
Tennessee, Ohio, Louisiana, Indiana, Mississippi	20	July 4, 1818
Illinois	21	July 4, 1819
Alabama, Maine	23	July 4, 1820
Missouri	24	July 4, 1822
Arkansas	25	July 4, 1836
Michigan	26	July 4, 1837
Florida	27	July 4, 1845
Texas	28	July 4, 1846
Iowa	29	July 4, 1847
Wisconsin	30	July 4, 1848
California	31	July 4, 1851
Minnesota	32	July 4, 1858
Oregon	33	July 4, 1859
Kansas	34	July 4, 1861
West Virginia	35	July 4, 1863
Nevada	36	July 4, 1865
Nebraska	37	July 4, 1867
Colorado	38	July 4, 1876
North Dakota, South Dakota, Montana, Washington, Idaho	43	July 4, 1890
Wyoming	44	July 4, 1891
Utah	45	July 4, 1896
Oklahoma	46	July 4, 1908
New Mexico, Arizona	48	July 4, 1912
Alaska	49	July 4, 1959
Hawaii	50	July 4, 1960

Glossary

adopt   to officially select something

assassinate   to kill someone, especially a political leader, by a sudden violent attack

banner   flag of a country or military group

bombard   to attack an enemy intensively with artillery fire or bombs

breaking trail   creating a new path where there was not one before

cabinet   group of senior officials appointed by a president to advise on policy

canton   rectangular area in the top corner of a flag, next to the staff or pole

Canton   Field

command module   part of a spacecraft that houses the controls and the crew's living quarters

composite   made up of different parts

distillery   place where strong alcoholic liquors such as whiskey, vodka, and gin are made

emperor   man who rules a large area consisting of many territories

field	background surface or color on which a design is displayed, for example, on a flag, coin, or coat of arms
flagship	vessel from which the admiral or unit commander controls the operation of a fleet
fray	to wear away the edge or surface of cloth, causing threads to hang loose
frenzy	state of uncontrolled activity, agitation, or emotion, such as rage or excitement
frigate	fast square-rigged fighting ship in the 18th and early 19th centuries
lunar module	small spacecraft used to travel from an orbiting command module (see separate entry) to the surface of the moon and back
masthead	top of a vertical pole that supports the sails on a ship

Flagship

69

merchant ships	seagoing ship designed to carry goods, especially for international trade
might	great power
parallel	relating to lines or rows that are always the same distance apart and therefore never meet
patriot	someone who proudly supports or defends his or her country and its way of life
pharaoh	ancient Egyptian title for a ruler of Egypt
planter	someone who owns or manages a large estate or farm
proclamation	public or formal announcement
representing	acting or speaking on behalf of one or more people
secede	to make a formal withdrawal of membership from a country, organization, or alliance
sledge	large sled pulled by animals used for transporting loads across snow or ice

Pharaoh

sloop	single-masted sailing boat
stern	rear part of a ship
surrender	act of declaring to an enemy or opponent that he or she has won and that fighting can cease

Sloop

tread	to control people's freedom by force
truce	relating to an agreement to end any kind of dispute or military hostilities
upholstery	relating to the craft, trade, or business of fitting chairs, couches, and similar items of furniture with stuffing, springs, and covering
widow	woman whose husband has died and she has not remarried
wiry	slim but muscular and strong

Index